GIRL ON A CORRUGATED ROOF

GIRL ON A CORRUGATED ROOF

ERIN SHIEL

RECENT
WORK
PRESS

Girl on a Corrugated Roof

Recent Work Press

Canberra, Australia

Copyright © Erin Shiel, 2023

ISBN: 9780645651232 (paperback)

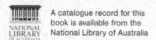

A catalogue record for this book is available from the National Library of Australia

Cover image: John Wolseley. *When the wind stopped* (detail) 2004–5, watercolour carbonised on paper. Private collection. Reproduced with persmission

Cover design: Recent Work Press

Set by Recent Work Press

Author photograph by Hellene Algie

recentworkpress.com

LB

For Robert, Liam, James, Jonathon and Matthew

Contents

Ghost girl

i

*That little girl runs like mercury let loose. She follows
me for a day every year or so. I've never seen her face,
just glimpsed her calves pumping like pistons up a ladder…*

The bunny

The t-shirt
was a gift
she didn't fully
understand. Pink,
tight and loaded
with a world of adult
mystery, the bunny
always made her feel
nauseous. She had seen it
leering from the bumper
bars of panel vans and trucks.

A hollow eye, a cocked ear,
no mouth from which to speak.

She wore it while she read
on the corrugated roof
that relentless January.
The iron was hot, the grooves
dug into her hips when she lay
on her side, but it was worth it
for the solitude. By the end
of *The Female Eunuch*
she peeled off the t-shirt
to let the Cassia leaves
dapple her skin, playing
with light and heat.
She had more to think
about than bunnies
on shirts.

On hearing my name

In the beginning, the name is what I am
told I am. Then I adopt it and it becomes
part of my own shape, a form to roll
around my mouth, a ball of clay, smooth

and cool. I grow, I learn, I say my name
like it's my own mantra. I take the name
to school and throw it in the playground
like a ball, to see if anyone will catch it,

throw it back or hurl it into the bush
behind the shed. It is comforting in
its roundness and soothing in its marble
cold. Then I grow pimples. I drive too fast.

I eat junk food late with friends. I get
a job I hate, pay rent, then a mortgage
on a house worse than the one I rented.
I love I love I love sometimes I hate.

I have a baby and I bring it home
to the house and the one I love yet
sometimes hate. I give the child
a name and say it to her over and over

until she catches the ball too and I see
her roll it around in her red play dough
mouth enjoying the cool. One day when
I am alone I go walking through

eucalypt forest. Cockatoos shriek
and the ocean can be heard through
the bush but not seen. Tiny finches
flit too fast for the eye. I almost tread

on a stick but mid-air I realise it is not
a stick but a brown snake and I hop
over it. It slithers into the undergrowth
flicking its body like a stockman's whip.

I walk deeper into the bush. A fog comes
in from the sea. From the distance it looks
like a shower curtain but it is too fine
to fall into rain. The fog creeps in between

the trees and bush. The finches have gone
home to sit and wonder in their labyrinthine
branches. The cockatoos are not shrieking
any more and I know this means the snake

has gone home too. There is no creature
here but me. I have a small torch. When
I switch it on the fog turns into a cinema
screen and I see it all: the house with

the mortgage, the argument with a lover,
the job I hate, the child I named, the friends
who made me laugh then cry, the bills
to pay, the unfixed crappy computer,

the aunt I haven't visited, the god I didn't
speak to, the course I didn't graduate from,
the meal I loved on the table I bought for
myself, the dress my father gave to me,

the book unwritten, the swim I didn't go for.
I brush my skin off scraping back with my
hands until there is just the fog and I,
the torch still shining, the light bouncing

off the fog as white as bed sheets. The bed
I made. Then I hear my name just once,
clearly. A bird calls it from within the fog.
I am in there. I hear myself for the first time.

Two red plums

Red plum in the fruit bowl.
It is the first of March. My teeth
make a satisfying crunch
as the golden flesh separates
from the stone. Bitter skin
takes me back to another Autumn.

She can only reach a fallen plum.
The juice runs down her neck
and wrists. She is wearing her good dress,
the one with the daisies on the end
of green ribbons. She throws
the stone at the black cat

who jumps, skittish, shaking
a back leg. She runs and hugs the cat
too hard. Stands up and sucks
her dummy, watches the Koi
in the pond who dash
out of her reach as she climbs in.

She slides on the weed and fills
a plastic bag with muddy water.
She can hear through the house
a knock on the front door. Adults are talking.
She listens. Still. She climbs cautiously
out of the pond.

She rubs at the mud on her dress.
        Puts the dummy back in her pocket.
   I take another bite out
        of today's plum.
      But the plum in my memory
           is finished.

How many hours did I spend
        amusing myself with a plastic bag,
   a cat and a fish pond?
         Next Autumn,
      when I eat a red plum
            I won't remember today…

but I will remember the fallen plum, the fish pond and the unexplained voices.

House pallet

Cracked Royal Doulton figures unable to be identified except possibly one of elegantly dressed woman in yellow observing a cuckoo and an old English character selling balloons maybe in Drury Lane, two giraffes, one spaniel and a horse. Several china vases never having carried flowers. Cloud layer of indiscernible emotion causing china pieces to hover above the next layer. Deconstructed glass and rosewood china cabinets for containment of figurines listed above inter alia. Layer of gravel composed of pebbles of jewel colours interspersed amongst the white from driveway of house. Layer of liver brick then layer of clinker brick. Cloud layer of frustration as clinker bricks didn't match liver bricks. Mattress with divots for hips and shoulders filled with petals from silk roses, dusted weekly. Layer of buttons, swatches of fabric, thread and needles and flattened toffee box where buttons were kept. Cloud layer of memories of child playing with button box at Laminex kitchen table making groups of like buttons into families. Laminex kitchen table. Layer of sixteen chrome legs and four red backs of chairs. Collection of Encyclopaedia Britannica. Layer of towels, sheets, pillow cases, face washers, doilies, dissembled vacuum cleaner. Drink coasters from pubs and bars. Layer of carpet, underfelt, dust, floorboards. Layer of broken bottles esp. milk bottles. Cake tins, casserole dishes, pots, pans, spoons, knives, forks. Deconstructed fridge. All empty except for a plastic polar bear mysteriously rescued from the freezer compartment. Square of ceiling plaster with grapevine in relief. Cloud layer of contentment when lying together on floor of newly completed house looking at grapevine. Bottles of pills, insulin needles, measuring devices, band aids. Cloud layer of pain. Lounge suite in burgundy brocade fabric dismantled with a chainsaw. Art Deco ashtray in chrome. Crystal diamond cut glasses and decanter in icy shards. Crushed toilet bowl. Crocheted toilet doll and unravelled spare roll. Knitted layette of deceased child. Dark cloud in thickened layer of its own that melts and permeates every layer like bitumen. Oak bedhead and end. Brown suit. Rose Guipure lace dress. Tan brogues. Navy court shoes. Stockings, socks, underwear enough for four days. Small bottle of Chanel no.5 perfume. A layer of letters, birthday cards, Form Guides, Christmas wrapping, bills and Tally Ho papers. Stratified cloud layer of arguments, unresolved issues, reflection and acceptance.

Captive audience

In the glass and rosewood china cabinet were royal doulton figures I admired
as a child, imagining myself doing the lambeth walk like the elegant woman
in yellow with the basket of lavender or wondering whether my mother looked
like the young girl in cerise that my nana bought on lay-by at david jones because

she was named marie. I fancied the girl called marie lived in a zoo and looked
after the animals. I would have looked after them with her but I was scared
of the noise of the china legs brittle against the glass shelf. When we slept
marie walked amongst the giraffes and horses. The baby giraffe was so sweet,

legs even more spindly than the white porcelain pony, they would both eat from
marie's hand and on Saturdays the pony gave her a ride. The spaniels would be by
her side as she did her rounds. Sometimes she stopped to buy a balloon from the kindly
old lady on drury lane. The yellow lady was her mother although she didn't seem

like the affectionate type. They were scared of a large fox that lived on the shelf above.
Gold leaf painted vases that had never held water were on the top shelf (sneak past
the fox): the castles that my girl and her lambeth walking mother retreated to when
they wanted tea and cake. The china cabinet was opened once a week for dusting.

They were always there for me to look at on long school holidays, to be dusted
with a retired singlet, to witness a daily ritual: the putting on of stockings; the broken
plates; the slow whistling; the cigarette rolling; the baked dinners. A captive audience,
an opera party with box seats, glasses to their eyes but never a hiss or bravo.

Sherbet on my tongue

Sans Souci Olympic Pool started
with a square box, a Tardis, squat
on the footpath gazing across
the Georges River. Iron stairs,
a clanging descent to the ticket

booth. Sherbet from translucent
packages spooned and spilled
into the mouths of cooler kids
with pocket money. Shuffling
thongs on wet polished concrete.

Chlorine wafted from the pores
of tanned pool bosses, leather
fish in crystal blue ponds. We ignored
the old river baths with their rusty
wire shark nets, their seaweed

and jelly blubbers. Rejected
for the gleam of the pristine
chlorine pool. On stinking hot
days Sans Souci Olympic Pool
effervesced at the end of the street,

zingy as sherbet on my tongue.

Payday

Friday afternoon my father
postpones his beer. Drives
to the contractor's house.
He grips the steering wheel
                with cement dusted fingers
                as he tells me he has laid five
                thousand bricks that week.
                I know my job is to sit in the front
and stare at the contractor.
He parks in the driveway, close
behind the contractor's car.
It is an ostentatious house,
                but not yet finished. A concrete
                crater of a swimming pool
                craves water in the side passage.
                The contractor is half naked, a towel
around his waist. My father
explains the ute will stay there
until he is paid. Cash. Or the watch.
I hear 'mortgage' and 'mouths'.
                He jerks his head towards me.
                I smile my school photo smile
                as I wind down the window.
                Then we wait. I clean out
the glove box. The contractor
emerges at sunset to hand over
a tight roll. My father winks.
Now there will be fish and chips.

Enough fabric to make a dress

Did you brush past me one night? When I was heading
to the thumping Marshall speakers to feel another sweaty
band transmit energy to my solar plexus, my *'little eagerness'*.
I think I was inspired by your fishnet stockings, twisted
white boots, worn the way you wanted to wear them.

Did my horse know your horse? I wandered the backlots
of my suburb until I found a horse I could borrow. A retired
racehorse. I had no idea how to ride but managed to get on
with a push. My denim on the saddle's leather. Once I was on,
the horse took off. I wasn't scared at all, just held on tight

and felt the exhilaration of height, power, thrust. I understood
your view from between the horse's ears. I loved all of your
fabrics, Jenny Watson, a whole Spotlight of cotton, stretcher,
satin, linen, velvet striped shantung, duck, Liberty, chintz,
hessian, corduroy, taffeta, netting, damask, (don't rain on my)

brocade, organza, vintage wool, antique silk, tapestry… Always
painting on enough fabric to make a dress to fit you. I wish
you had been there, when the priest lectured us in the classroom
on Friday afternoons while we girls were learning to sew.
I was leaking tears into the cross stitch on my dirty orange

gingham apron with canary yellow bias binding. He told us
all we needed to know was how to cook and sew. You would
have stood up and said something crazy to him in his black
satin cassock with the maroon cord trim and buttons. We could
have thrown our aprons out the window and gone horse riding.

The outsiders

They lumbered the station wagon
into a space under the gum. The dog

rose wearily to greet them, tail wagging,
then weeing on the tyre. The girl

pretended to sleep on the back seat.
Vinyl smell merged with Christmas

heat. Through the kitchen window
a punch bowl with cups hanging

from hooks clinked. Chattering voices.
Cackling laughter, then a quietening

as her father entered the back door.
She could see the spread with her eyes

closed. Trestle tables bowing with Bohemia
crystal bowls. Tomato and white onion

sliced in vinegar, pink ham climbing
out of its unfurled skin, pineapple slices

in lime jelly, a sweaty ambrosia of tinned
mandarins, marshmallow and coconut.

She remembered from last year the gossiping
spinster ladies from church lining the walls

and a handsy middle aged neighbour
dressed as Santa. She crushes her sundress

in fists, dragging down the shirring.
Her mother's face in profile was a mask,

the rarely used make up, jaw clenched,
eyebrows raised as her father came back

to the car. Hushed words at the wound
-down window. Some years he would smile

and nod, beckoning to them through the kitchen
door and they would prepare small talk

for the adults, presents for the children.
But today, he bombed into his seat, slammed

the door and screeched away to the sounds
of 'White Christmas' escaping from the radio

like air from a punctured red balloon.

The bridge

i

She's walking home after
the club, accompanied
by two beers and a fake ID.
The thump of the band
still shakes in her head.

Under the bridge   means choppy river waves
            like a mouth salivating,   lips considering a meal.
          Tides fumble   through the meeting   of the salt water
      and fresh   .   where tired and hungry sharks
            head back from up the river after birthing.

Past fishing hulls   suspended like dead whales.
            Scraped barnacles   crush under her feet.   A soldier crab
          scuttles from rock   to rock,   watching her
            tread on oyster shells   piled up
in layers of sand and silt   under the bridge.

She shimmies her shoulders   to bluff insouciance   but her stomach knots
            as she peers into bushes   where beer breath
swirling in her ear   would be the best
                  of what she might find.   A group of men grumble
and piss   behind scrappy bottle brush.   Could she swim

          to the pylon   in the middle of the river   is it safe there or is it a
trap?   One old bloke stops   to sing on the rocks.
          His pokies winnings fall from his jacket.   The coins spill like bullets
on the river.   She's seen him before,   harmless but no help.
          Ahead there's a scuffle,   juice bottle and hose bongs   are discarded

as she approaches.   They realise it's only her.   Turtle-headed boys in surf
       shirts emerge,   she wants to talk to them.
They have kind eyes but she knows   they're so stoned they can't speak,
         so they might feel her up instead. She likes them liking her   but she
doesn't want to be felt up.   Not this summer.   Though the loneliness is killing her.

She knows she's on the edge,
a little between radio stations
not quite tuned into the right
clothes, music, gossip. She pretends
to like what the others like, to fit in.
Here, on the river, it doesn't matter.
Now, she's got one toe in the salt water.

The chill feels electric.

               She's up to her neck.

                     It's like a rebirth.

                           Eight degrees, deep as a wound.

She's jumping out freezing,
dripping, running into the bush.
So far in, no one knows where she is,
even herself. Under the she–oaks
the needles beneath her flatten
the grass, no lawn can grow here.
No lawn but no snakes either.

ii

Over the bridge
feels different.
The top is a long
way from home,
from locked doors,
tissue box covers,

broderie anglaise,   ironed clothes and roast lamb. Safe so safe but the air seems
        thick with caution. Thick with warnings   and expectations. With 'as long as
you're happies' and   'when you get marrieds'. On the way up   the wind from
        rushing cars is cold   goose bumps rise from cool or fear.

A chill of discomfort   yet somehow fresh. She craves freedom   but she's terrified.
        There is no edge.   As she crosses the highway   her arms flail
like a newborn   unswaddled.   No-one there
                but petrol heads   in vans,   making her heart
                        pound in the dark.

Between street lights   she breathes faster.   Fresh and salt
        mixing in her lungs.   At the apex she swings   around the middle post.
It's always like that.   One minute she's terrified the next...
        Invincible. Leaning over the rail,   looking into the inky river
but knowing   the sharks swim below.   If she falls

she will be missing something.   There must be something to miss.
        Missing what? New clothes? A boyfriend?   A trip to Bali?
Friday nights at the Leagues Club,   trying to avoid the gropers?
    A chance to get a job as a receptionist.   Pretending to laugh
        at the sales reps' tired jokes? She'd rather read Plath,

but she doesn't know it yet.   From the top of the bridge the city twinkles.
        It used to be fairy land when she was little.
Now it's more ominous   than pixies with lanterns. But it's calling her away
        from lawns and fences,   petrol heads   her job at the chemist   trying new
nail polish every day.   Calling her away   from men telling her to learn

to sew and cook   because that's what girls are for.   Away from being shut down
        when she tries to talk about anything but make up, movies, boys.
Away from being told to *Smile*   by men who don't want her to talk.   Still, wanting
        the thrill   of touch   but not the emptiness of
        how many beers,   whose party,   who screwed who,

        which girl has bigger tits,   or gives better head.   Away.
The petrol heads   coming back from the club   can't get at her.
        They can't stop   on the bridge,
                where the speed limit is eighty,   and the road barriers are high.
They could wait for her   at the bottom when she walks home.
                But she might just never go.

Syzygy

A pendant light
in the hallway of a neighbouring
house was a standard joke on the evening
walk. Having escaped from the sky the moon hid
there. The father stopped, comic shock on his face,
looking at the spaniel and the girl in turn. 'Go on now,
chase that moon back up to the sky!' At five years old
she giggled. Over time this settled to a tired laugh. Then
a rolling of the eyes. Later again, it was just the two
of them, the spaniel wearily pulling the worn, red
lead when the father paused at the moon house.
It was a long evening walk, interrupted
by the sun of thousands
of days.

Ghost girl

ii

Onto the corrugated roof. Ponytail flying round a bend.
That little girl runs so I can't catch her. She dances heel,
toe, heel, toe under the calico dress. Bare feet even in snow…

Special care nursery

A mother sits in a moulded
plastic chair holding two
baby boys each lying
the length of her forearms.
She smiles as she imagines
them running
in a playground,
dirty faces,
snails in pockets,
her hands putting Band-Aids
on skinned knees.
But the knees she rubs
with one thumb
each are like cloves
of garlic, the pink variety,
unskinned, snappable
between two fingers.

Simryn Gill's pearls

*'I took a deep breath and listened to the old brag
of my heart. I am, I am, I am.'*

Sylvia Plath, The Bell Jar

Take a copy of *The Bell Jar*. Tear the cover
carefully from top to bottom like a zip. Skip
the front pages until you arrive at the text:
'It was a queer, sultry summer...' Rip each
page so the entire text is a pile of thin paper
strips. Take each strip and wind it. Watch
the heat of your hands and the moisture
in the air form it into a pearl. The words turn
around each other, forget rhythm or grammar
until they are reformed into a string of beads.

The winter I was breastfeeding my twins, I read
The Bell Jar as it balanced on my knees with one
baby pointing east and the other west. If I had
hung Simryn's pearls around my neck the text
would surely have soaked into my skin instead
of my eyes. The potent beads would have hung
over my heart down between my breasts,
babies and legs. *The Bell Jar*'s words are little
round pebbles. The strings are not tied into
a clasp, but lie loose, waiting to be finished.

Humble

I wave them off to school and turn to porridge bowls
and dirty clothes. My eyes search for one sharp edge.
The inside of the house shrinks, airless. I need flowers.
I walk out on Mount Stromlo to look for native daisies,

even bush pea. The field's full of paddy melons. Then,
a metal object, farm machinery, so honest against
the horizon. No artifice, no motive like a flower. I keep
searching for rusting detritus. Far easier than drinking

tea and tearing small pieces off iced buns avoiding talk
about stain removal and childhood illnesses. I bring home
weathered farm iron, road reflectors, soft drink crates.
He's not too sure about it yet. He works with stars,

constellations of gas, distant bodies he can't grasp.
All moon dust to me. My stars are sharp barbs on
rusted rolls of fencing wire. They twinkle with flecks
of zinc. My stars hurt, can be held, lie in dirt, lie in wait.

Too humble to shine or grant wishes. I bring together
crates broken into chunks. Word shards move in swarms
like insects chirring. Rain, sleet, wind, heat, pummel
surfaces humble. Remove the shellac, the slogan

of the drink company. Yellow and black road signs used
to giving directions bump together to form hills and valleys,
curve into each other like a child's jigsaw. See saw back
to Auckland. Garden knee deep in Michaelmas daisies.

Thank god my aunt painted the hydrangeas green.

Phoenix

She's a pop princess phoenix smelling of patchouli oil and Calvin Klein Obsession.
She spends her days lying on a chaise longue made of toffee and jewelled with fuchsia
anemones. She's solid but you can see through her if you look closely. She changes

her mind before your eyes, she's so malleable. Can you rely on her? You're asking
the wrong question. Who cares? She trills like a symphony of tambourine zills,
while dancing through a field of orange and pink gerberas. Lime green bees

distribute turmeric powder through fluffy purple straws. She's going under
to the otherworld collecting viscous slime in her hip flask. Sustenance for balmy
nights on stage, rising one more time to caress and carouse with her back-up

flock of neon caramel peacocks. Her ravishing song lights the flames of her rebirth.
One iris is magenta and the other tangerine, eyelids shadowed with seventies thick
turquoise blink soporifically at me. I wish I was reborn with some of her pluck.

Sink

I stand on a cliff and throw the hours
I've wasted into the ocean. They dissolve
to minutes then seconds amongst the buffeting

        waves. I dive in. Kick to the surface. The salt
        of tears buoys me as I float in the past. Each wavelet
        shimmers with memories I thought I had lost.

In the closest ripple I am back in our bathroom
on the first day I bathed my baby alone at home.
My forearm cradled his neck. My hand held

        his fist. His body startles then settles in the water.
        I felt so sure I could protect him. Yet the sink
        was as vast and cold as the ocean I swim in now.

Nacred

He arrives like a southerly. She ushers him in. Hungry
as he always was. They have three hours. She hurries
to lay a cloth on the table. She takes the butcher's paper
parcel from him noticing his ragged nails. Fingers with quicks
pulled yet the thumb a perfect shape so wide across
the hinge and square in the nail. They arrange plates
with lettuce and lemon wedges. Oysters, viscous clouds
sitting in the sea's two faced serving dish. Ceramic white,
jagged grey. The mollusc glistens and she remembers
the ocean pool. The effervescence thrust beneath
the surface by the curl and dump over the concrete edge.
He opens the bottle of Riesling she hands over. Twist twist
twist and pull. She knows nothing about him. The questions
would burst like bubbles if she asked them. Sitting at the table
the breeze through the kitchen window just cool enough
to summon up goose bumps. She snaps a mental picture.

> 'I should drop a grain of sand
> in one and wait for a pearl.'

> 'It's a parasite not a grain of sand. Irritates.
> Causes the nacre to form the pearl.'

They spend one hour eating, the other two in bed.
White sheets muddled as a rip current. Glasses
are empty. Oyster shells are bare. Lettuce wilted
to seaweed. Outer membrane of the lemon wedges
desiccated. He leaves and she sits staring at the remains.

> One day.

Swimmer

Standing on the blocks precise hands shake a rhythm.
I watch, anticipating a party trick, a bomb or a pencil.
Legs tensed, he keels into the water without a splash.
Stays in his lane, no switching between medium
and slow, no relaxing in splash and giggle
lap after lap just watching the black line
in the fast lane for years. He would know
where a tile is missing and the rust stain
near the twenty-five metre mark. Elbow
surfaces, pointing like a dogs' ear. Mind
drifts beyond the pool. At the end
of the first kilometre he looks up
eyebrow arched. Sweeps a curve
of water around him, noiselessly
considering the ripples, then
drops below the surface
testing his lungs
like a child

in the silent comfort of the water.

He knows once he leaves
the aqua refuge he
will need to listen
to the world.
Better keep
swimming.
He's found
his pace
with strong
deliberate
arm strokes

dividing the
water, like
scissors
cutting
silk.

Berg

Suddenly the waters around them slowly swelled in broad
circles; then quickly upheaved, as if sideways sliding from a
submerged berg of ice, swiftly rising to the surface.
Herman Melville, *Moby Dick*

There might be a peripheral memory
of his father sideways sliding into view
holding the back of a bike as he cycles off,
lifting him onto his shoulders, or spinning
him holding one hand, one foot. Around
the age he realises there's a world bigger
than home and the corner park, he hears
of his father's adventures on an icebreaker,
when he was away from home for work
or maybe in that submerged time when he

         was not yet born.

Like an old photo patched together,
we are a composite, two halves of parents,
four quarters of grandparents. But parts
of the scene are missing at the joins:
the porch of the home in which we grew up;
the people kind and cruel along the way;
the path we walked to school;
the dragonflies of an austral spring;
how family spoke to us at dinner. Forming
another plane in spray paint and graphite

        floating

in the foreground of us. Saturated
colour, not the blurry grey outline
of ancestry but our own self shaping,
vivifying the ice landscape we know
is there but not fully accessible.

The submerged berg of our character.
By staring out to sea, or the horizon,
by explorations of love and beauty,
work and duty the glacier of our history
calves at the hinge zone to form

                              our own ice floe.

Man child

Head hangs, fringe drapes, school
shoes unlaced scrape along the path.
A spark of energy opens the door

for a rush to the loo. Dismantles
the fridge for tuna and chocolate.
Bedroom door slams. He speaks

to someone. Animated conversation,
peppered with hammering guns
on a pixelated screen. The dog drags

at a putrid sock poking under the door.
Once, a lunch box growing mould
emerged. Then he wants a hug. It's like

holding a glass globe, carefully, but tightly.
It might shatter to splinters, leaving tired
hands to bleed in a pointillist pattern.

In Patricia Piccinini's workshop

It is late and she knows she should be home already as they were expecting her for an early dinner. Her car keys are in her hand but feeling the draught from under the workshop door she turns back, expecting an ambush or a party. The creatures are lying there quietly, cooing benevolently. She caresses each of them: their misplaced orifices, hair and crevices. But it is the hairy girl in the corner who she wanted to check on. She is the comforter and there are no limits to her love. She is glued to a glowing infant, an eyeless, earless, bonny baby with udders for hair. Patricia approaches cautiously and plays this little piggy went to market on the toes of the baby's stumpy feet. The baby laughs curling her lips and the gurgles ring out across the concrete floors and walls of the workshop. The udders on her head bounce. The comforter doesn't blink her synthetic eyelids but Patricia can tell from her calm demeanour that she is happy for the game to take place. It is clear from the girl's awkwardly pigeon-toed feet that she has slid down the wall to play with the baby. The baby has had enough of little piggy and turns away from Patricia. The girl and the baby cuddle and coo to one another. Patricia feels superfluous. Even excluded. She has nothing extraordinary in her physical appearance and her mundane features are unable to attract the attention of the cuddling pair. She blows them a kiss good-bye and backs out, looking forward to retreating home, where they wait for her, watching the clock and tapping their fingers on the table. The pair are quiet while the door closes. They snigger a little, then turn back to each other.

I need to tell you about the first time I saw snow

There were seven of us - my husband and I, my brother, his wife, their two daughters and my son. We needed two cars. On the way to Jindabyne granite boulders lay in the fields like sleeping dinosaurs. The first snow looked like a pool of spilt milk solidified on straw. The children were waving to each other from car to car and pointing as they saw new patches of snow. We were telling them to calm down and put their seat belts back on. My husband was a bit angry but he wanted to enjoy the holiday and his smile could not hide for long. We stopped at Jindabyne by the lake that was draped across the valley like a bolt of blue silk. My brother took a photo of my husband, my son and I. This is important. The children wanted to sit together on the way to Perisher. My husband and I were alone in the car without our son. It was so quiet our ears felt numb. Past Jindabyne along the Alpine Way our lights beamed through falling dark. We watched the two cars collide and jerk into the banks of mounting snow. I slid as I ran on the ice. The two girls whimpered in the back. I couldn't look at my brother. His wife wouldn't tell me where my son was. I kept staring into the reddening dark of the car. Someone I don't know put a picnic blanket around my shoulders. I kept saying 'three children in the back, two girls with my boy in between'. They walked me to a cloud of steam forming on the road. Thrown through glass to ice, I felt his cheek's last glow.

That's the first time I saw snow.

Chiaroscuro

They had spent hours lying in the sun
looking at their bodies, skin darkened
by angles of limbs: calf folded against thigh,
forearm resting on chest. Bodies were forms
catching light here and not there, playing in

and out of crevices, crevasses. As teenagers
they had their own darkrooms, exposing,
fixing, pegging prints in solitude. Later
they shared darkrooms to develop together,
edging around each other in the tiny space.

In one photo he is lying on the sand as sun paints
the insides of his eyelids blood red. His mouth
opens, acting surprised. Olive's shadow falls
on him. Her head bends over a Rolleiflex camera.
His effulgent torso and her shadow are one figure.

Their elbows make handles. His hands could cup
her breasts. What is she wearing? Is she smiling?
Once she photographed him after surfing, covering
him to the muscle above his hips, skin dry,
hair wet. What happened after the photo?

Shadows lack details, the viewer fills them in.

Whirring

The lover circles
his own heart
-Rumi

He
peers
through
the crack
and sees only
a dark room but
hears the whirring.
He has been warned.
He bites a wet lip and enters.
Now he is a voyeur to the dance
without a dancer. Maybe a solo or maybe
a pas de deux, he cannot say. He fears the chirring
in his ears until he wants to become part of this trance,
this lovers' dance. He feels his heart booming a rhythm that
melds with the blur and finds his feet following further into the room.
Circling the skirring silk. Watching for hours, finally he sees it for what it is.
A chance to escape the bewilderment of the days that remain.

I have never entered this room before. The air is damp and the walls have a crumbly feel, breaking up beneath my fingertips. They told me not to look in here. There is a rushing sound and a sense of desire winging by. I hear the caretaker running down the corridor and he rushes to my side. Flustered he implores me 'Look at the wall beyond. Use your peripheral vision.' The caretaker says it was the instant of the winter solstice when they first fell in love and as time stood still they locked together as a dance not dancers, love not lovers. When time ticked again they moved too fast to be seen but should a poet visit time slows and they can be glimpsed. 'Don't look too close. You might see their eyes.' I want to stay and drink in the coolness of the breeze their dance creates. The world outside continues for a week, a month, a year. The caretaker reminds me daily that the longer I stay the harder it will be to exit. I am unable to leave the room yet I am not part of their dance.

Ghost girl

Once when I scratched the back of a mirror, silver paint
flaked to reveal glass. A sliver of her grey eye stared back
at me. Her history is mine, hiding. In my sight's periphery…

The bolt hole

for Dette Ryder and Rose Walsh

Only the boys were allowed to swim at the bolt hole. Stripped
to their underwear, skin pale against the moss, they would weave
bulrushes to make a buoy across their goose bumped chests,
launch themselves from the bank and into the river under
the spray of the waterfall. This was the place where the salmon

swam upstream to the reddy pits to spawn. Springers till June
then the grilse run. They stroked to the centre of the river
their bulrush floats itching at their armpits. The salmon brushed
past their legs. Standing still as the willow on the bank the boys
could catch a salmon, clapping it between their hands as it tried

to jump the dam. The dam is gone now, pulled away to restore
the flow of the river. The boys are now rimpled old men battling
aches and the 'dying of the light'. The bulrushes are being counted
in a study. One of the old boys lies in bed, working out how
to roll over without hurting. He thinks of that salmon, swimming,

jumping up but not making it over the dam. Again and again
she stabs herself on angled twigs but she makes it over.
She continues through eddies, around rocks, until she finds
where she herself was hatched. She swishes her tail
in the gravel to dig a pit to lay a thousand eggs. The salmon

always returns home, led by olfactory memory. Not so these old boys,
they built bridges and dams in a new world. They returned home
once for a funeral but found no rest so left again to live alone
in flinders street boarding house rooms, eating soup and tuna
from cans. Their olfactory memories are of peat fires, woodbines,

soda bread, maybe the dank smell of sweat and wee when sharing
a bed with little brothers, the blood of the pig drained for the black
pudding, the eel eaten when meat was rare. Nights in greying sheets
were viscous with silence. Their hands clapping above their faces
at old words in the dark: *When it's cold, fish slow and deep.*

Bird

He's between the flyscreen
and the wooden battens of the verandah.
I undo the screws to release him,
make an opening,
but he flaps his way down
further into his prison.
Blood jewels now appear
at the tender point where wing
meets breast.
I feel sick trying to free him
though I am not the one trapped.

Cat

catcher of birds
cruel hunter
young boys coaxed
you in as a stray
you have made late nights
working less lonely
been a warm
pillow on the couch
kept sick children
resting by sitting
on their bedside table
an ornament in motion
one lick at a time
you were a calm
presence amongst
small tornadoes
now your body lies
between my arms
on the steel table
plump and purring
though in pain
you look at me
I give the word
and the needle
goes into your kidney
you rattle a breath
the plumpness subsides
until I could wring
out your body
like a black towel

Private lessons

Walking in the heat with the vinyl guitar case banging against her legs.
Resting against the gum tree to consider the remainder of a sandwich.
Outside the house standing on the cool verandah.
Dogs yapping. Door opens.
Follow him down the hall that smells of Old Spice.
The strings twang and hurt the fingers.
I'll teach you how to hold the guitar Spanish style.
Put the rounded bottom between your thighs. Open your legs.
Hem too high. Thighs stick to wooden chair.
His tweed pants too stretched. That's it, Lovely.
Need to go to the bathroom.
Small brass slide lock is stiff but push it hard.
Maroon and ochre tiles. One or two tiles green.
Exactly four tiles green.

Breathing.
Nothing to say, nothing to remember, nothing to tell.
Breathing.

Need to go to the bathroom.
Small brass slide lock is stiff but push it hard.
Maroon and ochre tiles. One or two tiles green.
Exactly four tiles green.
His tweed pants too stretched. That's it, Lovely.
Hem too high. Thighs stick to wooden chair.
Put the rounded bottom between your thighs. Open your legs.
I'll teach you how to hold the guitar Spanish style.
The strings twang and hurt the fingers.
Follow him down the hall that smells of Old Spice.
Dogs yapping. Door closes.
Outside the house standing on the cool verandah.
Resting against the gum tree to vomit up the remainder of a sandwich.
Walking in the heat with the vinyl guitar case banging against her legs.

Mettle

Three seats in the cabin:
one for the Driver,
one for the person who picks through the clean-up heaps,
one in the middle for the boy.

Not covered like a lorry. Messier
than a ute. The drop-sides are home-made.
Corrugated sheets collected kerbside.
The cabin smells of sweat and rust.

A fly crawls over his forehead.
His mother swishes it away,
curves her finger around his chin.
She climbs out and kicks at the edge
of a pile. Sodden pillows, a dirty
mattress, a burnt out stock pot.
The Driver stares at her. She zips
up her jacket. 'Wha's in the box?'
he yells and points, 'In the BOX.'
She drags a wet cardboard mess
from under the mattress. A drill kit.
'Leave the fuckin' drill, get the drill bits.'
He slides out to look at a wine rack.
Rips the iron carcass off the wooden
base and throws it into the truck.
'Like that. Don't waste time. I told
you to stay in the truck you little shit.'
The boy fingers toy cars in an ice cream
container. A fire engine slips into his pocket.

All three climb back into the seats in the cabin:
one for the Driver,
one for the person who picks through the clean-up heaps,
one in the middle for the boy.

Warm almonds

After they have eaten their home cooked
    noodles, they count out three almonds for each person
        in the office that day and warm them. An aroma wafts like incense
    from the little staff kitchen. They take turns at walking by the desks of each
of the counsellors, busy listening to tearful families.
    The plate is extended wordlessly. Never have almonds tasted
        so good, prepared with a seasoning of kindness.
    The gentility of the quiet accountants always strikes me as a gift
                        where we least expected it.

Love and the aged care worker

If she feels down, she walks by the river.
There she smiles at a cormorant
stretching its wings like a triplet
on a stave. Ragged as her own arms,
ready for caring, carrying, cleaning.

It's night shifts at the nursing home
this week. She's used to the stippled
sleep after lunch. The chiming of children
on their way home from school permeating
dreams, jemmying in reminders of young life.

At midnight she stands at the sliding
doors in the foyer looking for space junk
with Keith, a regular sundowner. They talk
about the children in her dreams. Keith says
'those kids are my friends at school.'

When the residents are feeling boxed-in
they discuss country towns in New South Wales
over tea and scotch fingers. They look
at a collection of souvenir spoons and talk
about camping trips or visits to farms.

At Beauty Time she's disarming in her choice
of nail polish for ageing fingernails. 'Go on,
try lime green! Look at mine?' The girls giggle.
'My husband likes pink on me.' one says.
'He's long dead so don't worry.' quips

a less forgetful resident. Quiet tears follow.
Then some reminiscing. Hands are massaged,
Pretty in Pink polish applied. The tears settle.
She catches everyone's shadows if they trip
over themselves, she runs when she hears

Eileen's gasping breaths down the hall. Strokes
her hair and talks about when her children
visited while they wait for the lifting hoist.
Eileen doesn't talk but her listening is intense.
Help arrives. She pries off Eileen's hand.

On Friday she drops in for Happy Hour,
though she's not rostered on. The Karaoke
machine is pumping and she sings 'I Am Woman.'
Helen Reddy would be proud. She is roaring.
She pats their hands as they say 'And Doris Day?'

She knows about sunrises viewed from behind
locked doors. It's not about the individual sunrise
but how lucky they are to have witnessed another
one. She bathes Keith at the end of her shift.
Mutters to herself: 'gloves first, gown, mask last'

as she leaves, stripping off and sanitising before
meeting her husband. Walk, nap, eat, work, repeat.
On Sunday nights they go to the supermarket before
the roster starts again. They shop for themselves
and both of their elderly mothers, wheeling two

trolleys like a precision driving team. Standing
near the empty rice shelves he takes her hand.
She flinches. Then remembers they live together
and grabs it, delighting in their shared skin, his palm
sealing leather against hers, shopping pleasure.

Drive by

They call, telling me to go
to the window. I part
the curtains to scan the street
for the car. The clock ticks
behind me. They are early
today. It's glistening in the front yard. Jacaranda leaves feather the sky.
Sunlight paints a gloss
on the magnolia I planted
last Easter. I can almost
smell the rain soaked
soil. This daily scene
is edged in black outline like a perfect picture coloured by a young child.
The car crawls into view,
no lights or sirens on.
Even the engine is silent
behind the glass. Where
are the neighbours?
The car window slides down. A young officer sticks her head out. She looks
up at me and I wave like
a snail's antenna. She looks
at a photo on her screen.
Nods a perfunctory smile
and aims her phone, taking
a snap of me pressing the pane. It's like a drive by shooting, only I am still standing.

Hand surgeon

He turns the boy's hand
back and over feeling each

joint and bone. More useful than an x-ray.
Only hands can fix hands the way diamonds
can cut diamonds. He holds the thumb

affectionately, the ugly cousin, stumpy and awkward.
Yet indispensable in its opposition. But he loves all the digits
and the way that hands, like Swiss army knives, spring

tools for screwing, scratching, sensing. Tacked
on the wall there is a photograph, surrounded
by his framed degrees—a pudgy toddler's hand

waving in the sun, scarred
but whole. Thanking, without
words, as only a hand can.

Ode to a container ship

Lying on your deck we have envied your life. A workhorse
among show ponies, you glide past ferries, cruisers and spindly
yachts. At the dock we see you load Lego boxes like a smuggler
on speed. No champagne is broken over your bow

but you toil all year bearing goods that grubby hands
grasp, hiding powdery substances in concealed
chambers. Your loads are awaited by child and crim alike.
We see the crew lavish affection on your sub-aqua

innards: paint them a colour (not grey) to conceal the clanging walls,
decorate with posters of tits and furry bits, photos and sports
fixtures from many ports. They know the comfort of your steely
bowels, the rhythmic creaks of your iron rooms made safe

by clank of bolt on hinge. Away, away so far away from feuds,
debts, faces. You are in your metallic element past the heads,
dividing the wind. Waiting outside Port Kembla you compare your
height to the escarpment. High cliffs softened by bush a perfect

vulva for your hardened bow. Keeper of the horizon, at dusk
you are a minus sign in the equation of sea and sky.
Reluctant advocate for refugees using plastic bags for pillows
and night's black velvet for a blanket, you have hidden us

in your 'tween decks, let us pray in your vast boxes. You ignore
borders we crave to cross. Our eyes scale your dizzying sides
and our frantic quest tampers with your disconnection from rocks
and soil, trees and territory. But, you ask no questions.

Elegy for a grocer

You do not have to be good
but when the longest day
sets it turns out it is better
to have been kind.
When Jack Hegarty died
and the skies were silent
with nostalgia and gliding
pelicans they lowered him
into the grave among
the rows of graves all flat
as the sea level earth.
No angels trumpeting
no crosses scratching
at the scurrying clouds.
Behind the mourners
a hunched man cried out:

'God bless you Jack Hegarty you fed us when we were hungry.'

His voice blew like the wind
and scattered its small vision
on our heads. Looking
at the dug soil we all
saw an image of you
in the corner store,
a tobacco paper stuck
to your lip, giving a nod
and a wave to the man
standing at the door
shifting weight from
one foot to another
clutching a paper bag

with one hand. The other
hand underneath
to keep it from breaking.

Dusk

A long table is set among the sheoaks,
            wooden chairs at varying angles
                echo the conversations
of yesterday. One is tipped backwards
      on the grass like an upended beetle
        an argument finished.
         Two chairs are tipped forward with the backs on the table,
flirting, a shared secret.
Your chair angled to mine,
      arms and legs touching.
      The dusk sky stretches a murmuration of starlings
     to breaking
       point.
      Like time's minutes, they work together
to expand and contract. We could have a day,
    we could have a year.
   On the table the bowls are not cleared,
     but almost empty.
        A fly clings to a scrap
       of wilted lettuce.
        A smear of cheese
      has hardened to yellow chalk in the sun.
  I have hidden since you left. Biding here, making a bed
on the dropped sheoak needles, covering myself
      in a blanket woven from leaves and numbness.
From above, the boobook chides me
    for overstaying in the dimming world.
        I know her call so well but I have never
          seen her face.
     Better to be out here,
where there are shades
     of dark. I can't stare

from inside the house, looking
for what was under the sheoaks.
From inside, grief hustles
against the window
turning the pane opaque.

Cabbage moths

My father's words
flit like cabbage
moths around

          his whitening
          head. His mouth
          opens and closes

as they escape
until there is a flock
of them. Wit waits

          a yard out of reach.
          'Well now, let me
          think...' he grasps

for the moths.
One he catches
in large warm

          hands. He slips
          it back into
          his mouth but once

caught it is dead.
Its fluttering wings
fail to convert

          to sounds, silvering
          his fingers but not
          his tongue.

Who are these bees?

I shelter from sleet
under a tree flowering
in the cold of December.
Ivory buds dangle like grapes.
They'll turn to fruit, I guess.
But I don't know this valley,
this country. I don't recognise

this tree, these out of season blooms.
How do they survive frosts and snow?
I won't be here to see the fruit.
The buzz above is deafening.
How many bees are here to make
this sound thick as honey?
I count only three fat, hovering sugar plums.

What a noise three bees make
in an unknown tree,
around an unknown flower
they're helping to fruit.
This is how they spend
their beneficent lives
in this quiet valley.

My mother, balancing

On the first day of my mother's first job the boss
sent her out at lunchtime to order a toasted ice cream
sandwich. All the men in suits thought it was funny
when she came back with the sandwich dripping
through the paper bag onto her white gloves.
At her second job she got married and they held

a farewell party. But I don't want to leave, she said.
They thought that was odd. My mother's work was at a desk
with a large accounting machine with so many keys.
It had its own rhythm that I never understood. Cha Cha Cha.
She was always racking her brain for a missing invoice payment
of $36.20. At her third job she was allowed to work even though

she was married. When I was born they delivered the accounting
machine to her house so that she could find the numbers
that weren't quite right while I slept to the Cha Cha Cha.
She had rubber thimbles on her thumbs so she could flick faster
through the papers looking for that number that wasn't right.
She made friends at work. They shared recipes and diets

and stories about their children putting plasticine in their ears.
They paid each other's children 50 cents on school holidays
so they could keep them quiet and bring them to the office
to file or organise rubber bands. In the lunch hour they rushed off
to the supermarket to shop for dinner or school lunches.
.... Mince.... Oranges.... Bread.... Milk....

My mother's job was before work too. She would dust the house,
put a casserole in the crock pot and hang the washing on the line,
cracking in the wind. The cold singlets would flap in her face
as she said her prayers. She said it was the only time she had to pray.
The magpies and the cat hung around her feet until they were fed.
At her fourth job in the furniture factory, when she did overtime

she asked for cash but received diamonds and shares in uranium
mines instead. She sold them quickly to pay for my school
uniforms. When she lost weight she admired herself in the window
of her office causing trouble on the factory floor below as the workers
stopped making chairs to whistle. She walked over the sewerage pipe
at the Botany wetlands to save on bus fares. I remember lying in bed

watching her do her hair for work, still a bit sleepy and loving her
scent swishing by my bed. Twist, twist, twist it up into a beehive.
Tweed skirt, twin set. Perfect for the office that is air-conditioned
for men in suits. At her fifth job my mother paid doctors' wages
and minded kids with disabilities so their mothers could have a break
and go to the hairdresser. She still managed to balance the books.

When she retired, the women she taught to balance books came
to visit her. There were funerals of the women who had taught her.
She found that missing $36.20 in the shower. In her mind she saw it,
in the wrong month. The credits and debits fell into place
and she felt easier. But that was just one part of the rhythm restored.
There was the mortgage too, the school fees, the meal planning,

the lunches for my father, the trolley shopping, the jibes from tuckshop
mothers about her latch key child. The day off when the child was sick.
The saving for the trip to see the in laws she had never met. The shiny
bloke in the office who made sleazy comments. The boss who kept
a second set of books. Her father's angina tablet prescription, clutching
at her heart. Her mother who needed help choosing carpet… Cha Cha Cha…

Red in the brain

A head clearing walk interrupted
by dogs and rain tussling together
to make a smell like old cars.

The dogs dive into the drains filled
with today's downpour, tannins,
twigs, a chip packet and a doll head.

At least the trees are a soothing
green punctuated by two reds
so alike I can't tell them apart

until I put on my glasses:
one a bottle brush flower,
the other a king parrot.

An old painter once told me
there's too much red in the green
of your front door. I've never

been able to see green
in the same way since,
now invaded by its opposite

like my brain struggling
for a metaphor but drowning
in anxieties of no value beyond today.

Coppiced

I have looked through the kitchen window
to the snow gum a thousand times, loving

the asymmetrical curve of its glaucous leaves
and its lignotuber, stocked with dormant life.

The secret the bush has written is in the insect
scribbles on this parchment bark. Yet until today

when speaking to my father on the anniversary
of his burial, I have never noticed that lichen

grows best on branches that are dead. New
shoots push out from coppiced stems.

Ringtailed

At dawn your fur brushes
        the sides of the roof above me. A limb bumps
then settles again in a corner. The day unfolds beneath you.
          I want to bury my face in your cream bellied comfort,
        hide with you in that dark
                cavity in my head.
Daylight pierces your eyes, sharpened by the corrugated
edges of the roofline, but you are unruffled, you close into yourself. I bang
        on the ceiling with a broom handle
          leaving dents in the plaster palate.
I can't get you out and night falls.
It seems an eternity since you inhabited that space.
                You have eaten all of your own excretions.
You wake. Slide your limbs under the skull edges,
flatten your fur against the iron eaves.
In the moonlight you have grown, your furriness expanding
        until remaining in the corner seems ludicrous.
What do you have to say?
Can you make anything happen?
        You explore the dusky
         world, feeding on the youngest leaves,
          leaping from trunk to trunk and scaring the dog,
so patient on the deck.
Just when I think you are out for ever,
    you chase across the roof,
      a bandit on the run,
      squeeze back in through my ear canal.
        I can never sleep
        while you are here. Never wake
          without wondering
           where you went.

If I leave you in the roof, thinking
we could understand each other,
you will ruin me. You will scratch
at the insides of my windows.
My eyelids will bleed from your clawing.
Desperate to feed your child,
I know, possum.
I know. Urine, excrement,
                    fur and blood left around
                              my every crevice.
Get out of my head. Say what needs to be felt
before I resort to a trap
                    with a wedge of apple and a tired carrot. I can't take you too far.
So tomorrow I know you will be back in my roof again. Nestling,
                    the ends of your fur fibres bristling
in my ear canal, stimulating me before the territory of night.

The ladle

Over years Lindy Lee has scooped and poured her thoughts:
snippets of days evaporating in her childhood backyard or sitting
at school cross legged, the concrete comfortingly hot underneath
her thighs while little blonde girls whispered and giggled on benches
nearby. Wisdom now runs like mercury in the furrows of her cupped

palms. Too many thoughts to hold. They leak through her entwined
fingers, bulge to break the surface tension at the edges of her hands.
The refractory furnace roars at the foundry. When the lid is lifted
the sound of fire escapes like liquid lava. Lindy lifts in each thought
cautiously, so the fire does not catch her sleeve. Then bars of bronze

are inserted. The lid is closed, thoughts and bronze meld to form
a viscous soup of sun-glow. Lindy spoons out the molten bronze,
honey lit with wisdom. She is strong but struggles under the weight.
The ladle is swung over a mound of sand on the foundry floor. Bronze
pours like toffee, could burn through to bone or take a tongue off,

still licked with flames as it drops into the sand. The sun-glow dulls
to a solid, the light extinguished as it cools to a tarnished symbol.
The energy of flung bronze is captured in the shape of the forms
in the same way a long walk shapes the thoughts of the walker.
The transformation, solid to liquid and back to solid again is part

of the meander. We find our shape, the limits of which are only
determined by how far we run and where our boundary's surface
tension will break. Like most art, it looks easy. To lift art to the angle
where we can be tipped from a ladle, flow to our limits, break
our surface tension, she has to work hard, and the ladle is heavy.

Syaw

It takes more than one day to weave a syaw
to catch a prawn's swimmerets, or the fin of a fish.
Time finds the gaps we've tried to ignore.

Over and under, over and under, the net forms.
Our mesh must be fine to trap a floating wish.
It takes more than one day to weave a syaw.

Some years it's easy to weave more and more,
yet some years we struggle with one loose stitch.
Time finds the gaps we've tried to ignore.

Some nets have patches and don't hide their flaws.
Other nets' seams have been sutured to vanish.
It takes more than one day to weave a syaw.

A net woven carelessly leaves an open door.
It's not just for fun, no net means no fish.
Time finds the gaps we've tried to ignore.

We strip the pinbin bush to weave the core
of days that form the years we cherish.
It takes more than one day to weave a syaw.
Time finds the gaps we've tried to ignore.

Ghost girl

iv

*She is there. Laughing when I miss her again. Iced breeze
announces her arrival. She crouches behind the lounge
when I feed my baby after midnight. Chilling me, she sings…*

Capers, falling into the ocean

White wings edged in black, like a cabbage moth
dressed for dinner. I read about the caper migration,
incrementally moving southward, onward, forward,
flitting up and down forming troughs and spikes

like a line graph of temperatures in November
before summer and the fires. A wave of black,
yellow and white. Sometimes they tap into a faulty
navigation pattern and fly straight out to sea alternating

between intended flight plans and a vague flutter,
then more flying, flying and then when land is out of sight
in all directions, no ultraviolet colours on flowers to catch
a butterfly eye, just waves and waves, then flapping,

flapping, in their search for a floating caper spinosa
flower on which to land. Fatigued, they fall into the ocean
to be washed into shore, a mystery for a sad child to solve.
Today I am stalled on a freeway that is free in no sense

of the word. I close my eyes, imagine the capers in my yard,
fluttering in the red and green of the callistemon, lighting
on the orange grevillea, landing wire legs on the mustard
kangaroo paw outside the back door. I open my eyes

to glinting silver and white, glistening metallic greys.
All on a bitumen canvas. As if it read my mind, there flitting
from one hot metallic surface to another, is a lone caper
butterfly. Once again, off course, although perhaps trying

to find a source of shrubs in which to rest. The map
imprinted in genetic memory doesn't feature this freeway
where once there were scrubby grasslands and shrubs,
nests for a thousand eggs where the bitumen is now.

Measuring silence

Rain falls onto the nasturtiums
in the cool of evening. Raindrops
roll over the waxed hairs of leaves
like quicksilver beads, then gather

together magnetically, forming
a diamond marble, polished
but no facets cut, no sharp points.
The marble magnifies the veins

on the leaf, finding the centre,
cradled in shallow plates until
a waft of breeze or even a sound
leads the leaf to tremble. The quiet

in the garden is so palpable,
that it could fill the rain gauge
and be poured back into the pond
drop by drop. Silence trickles

from sheoak needles and hushes
their whisper, it muffles each wave
rolling up from the beach at king tide.
The jirri jirri stops dancing to listen,

his tiny heart a slowing metronome.
He will not move, afraid silence
will fade to noise. Quiet quells
each leaf. Each frog's spawn rests.

The diamond marbles are still.
The silence around them meets
the surface tension of the water.
Pushing, yet being pushed in return.

A measuring instrument: one sound
will topple a marble from a plate.
Silence completes gaps between leaves,
birds, strands in the birds' nests.

When the wind stopped

Wolseley stands on the hill under
the scribbly gum looking over

           the scrub, eyes flickering over burnt
           bush. The trunks of the eucalypts
      kneel on a cushion of new green,
      dead arms extend up in praise,
         lemon myrtle their incense.
         He unrolls the paper and cuts
as though he's releasing a chained
creature, sliding the scissors

     through, feeling the smooth
     incision, wincing at occasional
       jags as the angle of the blade
       shifts. Ahead burnt out scrub
     follows the flow of the terrain,
     heights of the trees varying,
        limbs tracing the rise and fall
        of the land so from above
it is a carpet of foliage.
He releases the sheets one by one.

      They flap and fly over
     the scrub like cumbersome
        birds unaccustomed to catching
        the breeze. Feathered ends flay,
unfurl power but the wind
drops and the flapping

      settles into a glide until
     the sheets are caught
    by the reaching arms of the mallee.
     The charcoal stipples and
        scrapes a song on the sheets.
        They struggle,

flapping then wrapping,
settling to swaddle low
burnt out baby bushes.
The pages caress and
smooth the hangnails of
petrified twigs.
They stretch a fraction
to scratch their song.
The charcoal song pleases
Wolseley still standing on the hill.
He taps one foot impatiently. Leans
to one sheet of paper then
another before he dances
through the mallee chasing
them one by one.
He calms their scrimmage,
detaching them from
snags and twigs.
He carries them out of the wind
on his two outstretched arms back
to a clearing and lays them tenderly
on a carpet of red dust.
He sings the song the charcoal
scrawls have composed
and stills them with his voice.
While they rest he considers the ring
necked parrots screeching above.
How will he entice them
to land on the scroll
that documents the mallee song?

Chandelier

Where does a chandelier belong?

If an icy orb grows at the centre of a chandelier
will you think of an ostrich egg guarding a mosque
from spiders? Will you think 'That chandelier
does not belong here.'? Will you think of Antarctic
ice shelves or the lead content of crystal drops?
Maybe you will revel in the glisten of the ice
when the lights go on at dusk. If you have a guest
she could break off an icicle to use in her martini
as a swizzle stick. When dimmed the candles
will burn like dying embers of a campfire
or the warmth in the low sky at sunset
when day's blue is sucked to the moon.

Grace Bros Miranda Fair lighting department

In my childhood home, three bedrooms
and the lounge room had chandeliers.
Not purchased in bulk from the coffers
of a French noble, and lowered on feast
night to be lit with a taper by servants
scurrying before the guests arrived
to drink claret, eat pheasant and suckling
pig. Not made by Venetian artisans
in island workshops blowing bulbs
by mouth and twirling a rod in a hot
oven until the glass dripped like amber
sap. Our chandeliers were bought one
by one with five dollars saved from each
pay for the best part of the year I turned
seven. Chandeliers need flock wallpaper
to accentuate their luxury so my father
spent weekends lining up the patterns
of one strip with the next. The houses
of the brickies he worked with were lined
with opera house carpet, regent hotel tiles.
Our chandeliers were bought from Grace Bros
Miranda Fair lighting department.
On Thursday night or Saturday morning
we would visit the hot cave glittering
not with seams of gold quartz crystal,
or glow worms, but with chandeliers
(and their poorer, colonial style cousins
destined for country kitchens).

A thousand price tags dangled above our heads.

Magnolia

The chandelier of the garden
is the magnolia. Bare elegant
arms stretch to hold the lights.
Finial not above like a waiting
weapon but rooted in earth.
Each cupped hand holds a pale
green bobeche with a bulb
not yet open. Purple outer
sepals protect the luminous
petals within. The magnolia
chandelier could be hung
in the ceiling of a pre–dawn
spring night. Once bloomed
the petals will drop leaving
the stamen, an exposed
filament, orange with pollen.

The usefulness of a chandelier in Antarctica

Our igloo had always been admired for being both solid and translucent. On summer evenings when we'd come home after ice fishing, the candles on the dinner table could be clearly seen. The crystals which formed on the ceiling after a slight melt hung like stalactites and could be broken off for ice in drinks. Guests from the north were thrilled by this when we entertained. One night we were woken by the unmistakeable crack of an ice floe breaking off. Mum threw her anorak over her pyjamas and opened the window hatch. 'It's not any old ice floe, we are the ice floe!' she exclaimed with an unsteady mix of excitement and fear. We could feel the movement now, as if we were on a barge. We clung to each other wondering how to approach this floating crisis. Our training in Antarctic survival had not covered 'Igloo floats away as an ice floe'. Mum had a brainwave. Lighting a candle first, she disconnected the electricity. Climbing onto the rosewood table she yanked the chandelier from the ceiling and tied it around the supporting pier at the centre of the igloo. She swung the chandelier around her head like a lasso and threw it until it caught a passing ice boulder, candle arms sinking into the snow. The igloo ground to a halt. We were saved, secured to the mainland by an anchor in the shape of a chandelier. The crystal drops of the light fitting seemed at home with the snow and ice. Passing penguins stopped to consider the brass finial while we had hot toddies by candlelight watching our anchor. It was like being on a harbour cruise in Sydney in our pre-Antarctic days, our boat moored to a fairy lit harbour wharf.

Saffron thistle sticks

Saffron thistle sticks
bathed in shifting
light create
a pastoral patchwork
a piece to walk around

Light shifts
on a pastoral
patchwork of
saffron
thistle sticks
a peace to walk
around

Shifting light bathes
saffron thistle
sticks to create
a pastoral patchwork
a peace to walk around

Saffron light
bathes
a pastoral
patchwork
created by
shifting thistle
sticks
a piece to walk
around

Shifting thistle sticks
bathed in saffron
light create a pastoral
patchwork
a piece to walk around

Creating
a pastoral
patchwork of
saffron thistle
sticks in shifting
light
a peace to walk
around

Light shifts on
saffron thistle
sticks creating
a pastoral
patchwork
a piece to walk
around

Saffron thistle sticks create a
shifting patchwork bathed in
pastoral light
a peace to walk around

Saffron thistle sticks bathed
in pastoral
light create
a shifting patchwork
a piece to walk around

Bathing saffron
thistle sticks in
shifting light
creates a pastoral
patchwork
a peace to walk
around

Saffron thistle
sticks bathed
in pastoral light
create
a shifting
patchwork
a peace to walk
around

Bathing saffron thistle
sticks in shifting lights
creates a pastoral
patchwork
a piece to walk around

Saffron thistle
sticks create
a shifting
patchwork
bathed in pastoral
light
a piece to walk
around

Light shifts on saffron
thistle sticks creating a
pastoral patchwork
a peace to walk around

Creating a pastoral
patchwork of saffron thistle
sticks
in shifting light
a piece to walk around

Shifting thistle
sticks bathed
in saffron light
create
a pastoral
patchwork
a peace to walk
around

Shifting light
bathes
saffron thistle
sticks to create
a pastoral
patchwork
a piece to walk
around

Saffron light bathes
a pastoral patchwork
created by shifting
thistle sticks
a peace to walk around

Light shifts on a pastoral
patchwork of saffron thistle
sticks
a piece to walk around

Saffron thistle
sticks bathed in
shifting
light create a
pastoral
patchwork
a peace to walk
around

Gymea lily

Lying so long in the forest with no name, earth's
soul rumbling beneath her, mist steaming from branches
and trunks, dewing her sleeping limbs. She's waited
so long. Feeling the warmth generated by humus,
squeezing charcoal loam between her toes. Myrtle beech
roots are her bed frame, layered leaf fall her rumpled
linen. Her eyelids open to witness herself tumbling
up through the generous soil. She's waited so long.
Light sparks her red tepals, though her anthers reflect
the canopy. She's found her way to the sun. A shredded
heart, elevated above the shrub line on a thin, green pedestal.

Ghost girl

v

'It's my baby too' she sings. She cleaves morning from day,
afternoon from evening, year from year. If she turned around
what would I say? Always in the silvering time, that little girl runs.

Notes

Quote in epigraph is from Sharon Olds, 'Ode of Girl's Things' in *Odes,* Cape Poetry, 2016.

'On hearing my name' is a response to Aida Tomescu, *Obliqua*, 1997 in Laura Murray Cree and Nevill Drury, *Australian Painting Now*, Craftsman House, Sydney, 2000, p.289.

'House pallet' and 'Captive audience' are responses to Sean Cordeiro and Claire Healy, *Cordial Home Project 2003*, see images online at *The Cordial Home Project* at Claire Healy & Sean Cordeiro (claireandsean.com).

'Enough fabric to make a dress' is a response to various works by Jenny Watson. See images online at Roslyn Oxley9 Gallery.

Italicised words in 'Enough fabric to make a dress' are from Sharon Olds, 'Ode to the Clitoris', in *Odes*, Cape Poetry, 2016.

Quote before 'Simryn Gill's Pearls' is from Sylvia Plath, *The Bell Jar,* 1971, Harper, p.274.'Simryn Gill's Pearls' is a response to Simryn Gill, *The Bell Jar in Pearls,* 2008. See image in Simryn Gill, *Raking Leaves*, London/Colombo, 2008.

'Humble' is a response to Rosalie Gascoigne, *Monaro,* 1989. See image online at Rosalie Gascoigne Monaro, 1989; sawn / split soft drink crates on plywood; 130.5 x 465 cm – Roslyn Oxley9 Gallery. 'Humble' is a fictional representation of the early days of Rosalie Gascoigne's artistic development. The biographical details referred to in this poem owe a debt to the interview of Gascoigne conducted by Robin Hunter for Screen Australia Digital Learning as part of the Australian Biography project. See online at Australian Biography: Women | National Film and Sound Archive of Australia (nfsa.gov.au).

'Phoenix' is a response to Kate Rohde, *Phoenix Vase*, 2018. See online Obsessed: Compelled to make — Kate Rohde.

'Nacred' is a response to Cressida Campbell, *Oysters,* 1994 in Laura Murray Cree and Nevill Drury, *Australian Painting Now*, Craftsman House, Sydney, 2000, p.86.

'Berg' is a response to William Eric Brown, ATKA Series, see online William Eric Brown : Photographs & Works on Paper : ATKA Series.

'In Patricia Piccinini's Workshop' is a response to Patricia Piccinini, *The Comforter,* 2010 at Art Gallery of NSW. See image in Patricia Piccinini and Helen McDonald, *Patricia Piccinini, Nearly Beloved*, Piper Press, Dawes Point, 2000, p.154-5.

'Chiaroscuro' is a response to Olive Cotton, *The Photographer's Shadow,* 1935, in Helen Ennis, *Olive Cotton: A Life in Photography,* 4th Estate, Harper Collins, Sydney 2019, p.240. The biographical research of Helen Ennis is also acknowledged.

Quote before 'Whirring' is from Rumi, Jelaluddin, *The Lover Circles his own Heart* as quoted in Mary Knights and Ian North, *Hossein Valamanesh, Out of Nothingness*, Wakefield Press, South Australia, 2011, p.87.

'Whirring' is a response to Hossein Valamanesh, *The Lover Circles his own Heart,* 1993 at the Museum of Contemporary Art, Sydney. See image in Mary Knights and Ian North, *Hossein Valamanesh, Out of Nothingness*, Wakefield Press, South Australia, 2011, p.59.

'Ode to a container ship' is a response to Joe Frost, *Docked Ship,* 2005, see image at Watters Gallery Joe Frost.

'Elegy for a grocer' is a response to Tom Carment, *Angel, Waverley Cemetery,* 2009. See online at Damien Minton Gallery—Tom Carment.

The italicised words in 'Elegy for a grocer' are from Mary Oliver, 'Wild Geese', *Wild Geese Selected Poems*, Bloodaxe Books, 2004, p.21.

'The Ladle' is a response to various works by Lindy Lee: Moon in a Dew Drop MCA Exhibition, 2020-21 see Lindy Lee: Moon in a Dew Drop | MCA Australia.

'Syaw' is a response to Regina Wilson, *Syaw (Fish Net)*, 2005 in R. Ian Lloyd and John McDonald, *Studio, Australian Painters on the Nature of Creativity*, R. Ian Lloyd Productions, Singapore, 2007, p.246. A Syaw is a fishing net in the language of the Ngan'gikurrungurr people.

'Measuring silence' is a response to Cressida Campbell, *Nasturtiums*, 2002. See image at AGNSW - Cressida Campbell - Nasturtiums.

'When the wind stopped' is a response to various works by John Wolseley. For examples see Barry Hill and John Wolseley, *Lines for Birds*, University of Western Australia Publishing, 2011. The artwork *When the wind stopped* can be viewed at Roslyn Oxley9 - John Wolseley. A detail from this artwork has been reproduced with permission for the cover of this collection.

'Chandelier' is a response to various works by Nicholas Folland including *The Door is Open*, 2007 and *Anchor*, 2008 at Museum of Contemporary Art Sydney. See image at *The door was open...* by Nicholas Folland | MCA Australia.

'Saffron thistle sticks' is a response to Rosalie Gascoigne, *Piece to Walk Around*, 1981, Museum of Contemporary Art Sydney. See image in Glenn Barkley (et al) *Volume One, MCA Collection*, MCA, Sydney, 2012, pp 84-5.

Acknowledgements

These poems were written on Gadigal land. This land was never ceded. Always was and always will be Aboriginal land.

Let me express my deepest gratitude to my mentor, teacher and friend Judith Beveridge. Without her gentle encouragement and guidance this book would not have made the distance.

Thank you to Shane Strange, Lisa Brockwell and Recent Work Press. I feel so honoured to be on the list of poets this dynamic and dedicated publishing house has selected.

To my poetry group members, past and present, you are all present in these poems. You've grappled with my drafts, suggested words, punctuation, lineation and given me insights into what the poems meant when I haven't even known myself. I would like to acknowledge the support of the following poets: Mona Attamimi, Alexa Bates, Alison Gorman, Dimitra Harvey, Miriam Hechtman, Rob Lowing, Denise O'Hagan, Genevieve Osborne, Kate Rees, Tegan Schetrumpf. In their own ways at various points on this journey they have kept me going. I also owe a debt of gratitude to Kate Grenville and John Tranter, who kept me writing during the early parenting years. To the artists who have been so generous with their time, sharing of their thoughts on creative process, their incredible artworks and in John Wolseley's case, the cover of this book, thank you.

My parents Marie and Jim Shiel provided me with the ladder to get up on that corrugated roof. They were not sure why I was going there but trusted my instincts from a young age to let me run my own race. I am so grateful for the long hours they worked to provide me with the time and space to dream.

My family and friends have nurtured me, listened to my neuroses, read drafts, reminded me the creative journey was both necessary and valuable, minded my sons, covered for me at work when my head was in a poem, accompanied me to readings when I was too nervous to go on my own. There are many of you who have been wonderfully supportive, and you all know what you did to support me.

To Matthew, Jonathon, James and Liam, thank you for the inspiration you gave me every day as I watched you grow into the wonderful people you are today. I guess this book is like another super annoying sibling. Thankfully they have grown up too. I hope you can forgive them for being a pain.

And to Robert, who cradles my heart. No-one has listened, encouraged and read more than you. You believed from the first time I met you. And, unbelievably, you still believe.

I am deeply grateful to the editors of the following publications where poems in this collection have appeared:

'On hearing my name', video of reading at Spirit of Self Expression 2020 Live Poetry Reading – Verity La, September 2020.
'Two red plums' *Romanian Australian Poetry Anthology*, Palatul Culturii Bistri a România, October 2020.
'Special care nursery', *Not Keeping Mum Anthology for PANDA,* March 2020.
'Simryn Gill's pearls', *Australian Poetry Anthology,* Vol 2, 2013.
'Nacred', *Australian Love Poems*, Inkerman and Blunt, 2013.
'In Patricia Piccinini's workshop', *Cordite*, May 2019.
'Whirring' (Longlisted) *University of Canberra VC International Poetry Prize 2018 Anthology: Signs.*
'The bolt hole' (Shortlisted) *University of Canberra VC International Poetry Prize 2018 Anthology: Signs.*
'Cat', *Romanian Australian Poetry Anthology*, Palatul Culturii Bistri a România, October 2020.
'Hand surgeon', *Medical Journal of Australia*, March 2015.
'Ode to a container ship', *Alterity Studies and World Literature*, July 31, 2020 Issue 2–3.
'Who are these bees?' (Longlisted) *University of Canberra VC International Poetry Prize 2019 Anthology: Silence.*
'My mother, balancing', *Mascara*, December 2019.
'Syaw', *Meanjin*, Summer 2015.
'Capers, falling into the ocean' (Winner) *South Coast Writer's Centre Poetry Award Anthology*, 2021.
'When the wind stopped', *Cordite*, November 2014.
'Grace Bros Miranda Fair lighting department', *Mascara*, December 2019.
'Magnolia', *Cordite*, March 2016.

About the author

Erin Shiel's poetry is inspired by art, empathy and the impact these have on identity and daily life. Erin has had poems published in journals and anthologies such as *Mascara, Meanjin, Cordite* and *Australian Love Poems*. Her work has been shortlisted for the University of Canberra's Vice-Chancellor's Poetry Prize (2018) and the Blake Poetry Prize (2008). In 2022 she won the South Coast Writers Centre Poetry Award. She has worked in the health and community sectors, particularly in cancer prevention and early detection as well as in support services for children and families. She has a Master of Public Health, a Master of Arts in Literature and a Master of Arts (Research) from the University of Sydney. She is currently training to be a counsellor in the Master of Counselling program at the University of Notre Dame and is enthusiastic about the role of creativity and poetry in therapy. She lives with her partner and the youngest of her four sons on Gadigal land in Newtown, Sydney.

www.ingramcontent.com/pod-product-compliance
Ingram Content Group Australia Pty Ltd
76 Discovery Rd, Dandenong South VIC 3175, AU
AUHW020721050325
407891AU00005B/36